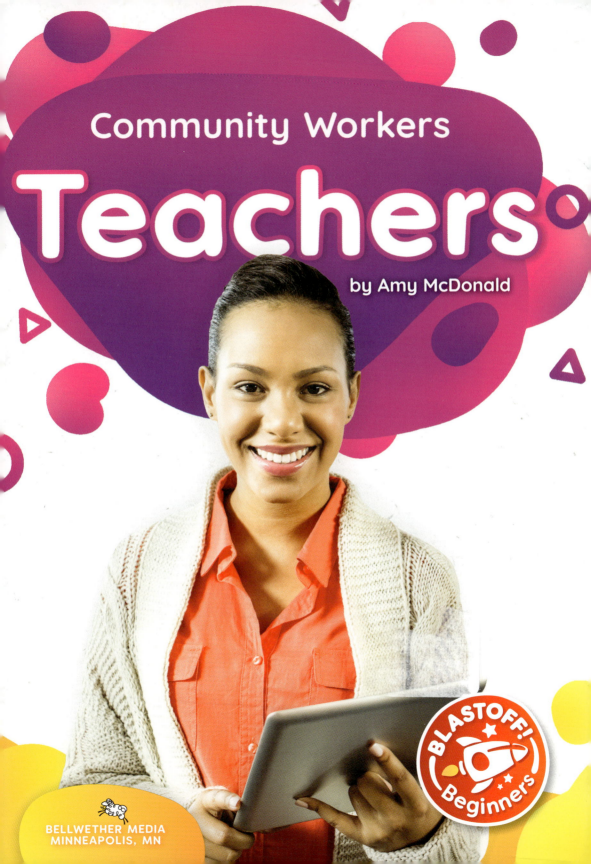

Blastoff! Beginners are developed by literacy experts and educators to meet the needs of early readers. These engaging informational texts support young children as they begin reading about their world. Through simple language and high frequency words paired with crisp, colorful photos, Blastoff! Beginners launch young readers into the universe of independent reading.

Sight Words in This Book

a	in	on	time
for	is	people	to
from	it	some	use
have	make	the	we
help	many	they	write

This edition first published in 2025 by Bellwether Media, Inc.

No part of this publication may be reproduced in whole or in part without written permission of the publisher. For information regarding permission, write to Bellwether Media, Inc., Attention: Permissions Department, 6012 Blue Circle Drive, Minnetonka, MN 55343.

Library of Congress Cataloging-in-Publication Data

Names: McDonald, Amy, 1985- author.
Title: Teachers / by Amy McDonald.
Description: Minneapolis, MN : Bellwether Media, 2025. | Series: Blastoff! Beginners: Community workers | Includes bibliographical references and index. | Audience: Ages 4-7 | Audience: Grades K-1 | Summary: "Developed by literacy experts and educators for students in PreK through grade two, this book introduces beginning readers to teachers through simple, predictable text and related photos"-- Provided by publisher.
Identifiers: LCCN 2024004945 (print) | LCCN 2024004946 (ebook) | ISBN 9798886870121 (library binding) | ISBN 9781644878491 (ebook)
Subjects: LCSH: Teachers--Juvenile literature.
Classification: LCC LB1775 .M3145 2025 (print) | LCC LB1775 (ebook) | DDC 371.1--dc23/eng/20240207
LC record available at https://lccn.loc.gov/2024004945
LC ebook record available at https://lccn.loc.gov/2024004946

Text copyright © 2025 by Bellwether Media, Inc. BLASTOFF! BEGINNERS and associated logos are trademarks and/or registered trademarks of Bellwether Media, Inc. Bellwether Media is a division of Chrysalis Education Group.

Editor: Betsy Rathburn Designer: Laura Sowers

Printed in the United States of America, North Mankato, MN.

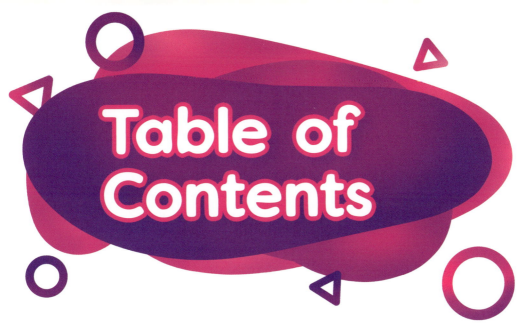

Table of Contents

On the Job	4
What Are They?	6
What Do They Do?	10
Why Do We Need Them?	20
Teacher Facts	22
Glossary	23
To Learn More	24
Index	24

On the Job

The bell rings.
It is time
for school.
Hello, teacher!

What Are They?

Teachers help people learn. They teach many subjects.

They work in schools. Some have classrooms.

school

classroom

What Do They Do?

Teachers plan **lessons**.

They talk to the class.
They write on a board.

They listen to **students**. They answer questions.

students

They grade work. They use computers.

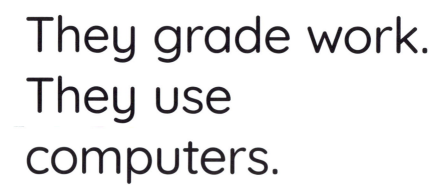

They plan games. They plan **field trips**.

field trip

Why Do We Need Them?

We learn a lot from teachers. They make learning fun!

Teacher Facts

Tools

computer

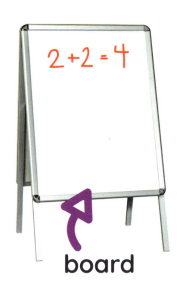
board

lesson plan

A Day in the Life

plan lessons

listen to students

grade work

Glossary

field trips
trips taken with a school

lessons
plans for teaching students

students
people who learn from a teacher

To Learn More

ON THE WEB

FACTSURFER

Factsurfer.com gives you a safe, fun way to find more information.

1. Go to www.factsurfer.com.

2. Enter "teachers" into the search box and click 🔍.

3. Select your book cover to see a list of related content.

Index

bell, 4
board, 12, 13
class, 12
classrooms, 8, 9
computers, 16
field trips, 18, 19
games, 18
grade, 16
help, 6
learn, 6, 20
lessons, 10
listen, 14
people, 6
plan, 10, 18
questions, 14
school, 4, 8
students, 14
subjects, 6
talk, 12
teach, 6
work, 8, 16
write, 12

The images in this book are reproduced through the courtesy of: wavebreakmedia, front cover; WML Image, p. 3; Monkey Business Images, pp. 4-5, 22 (listen to students), 23 (field trips, students); SDI Productions, pp. 6-7; B Brown, p. 8 (school); JohnnyGreig, pp. 8-9; Dark1elf, pp. 10-11; monkeybusinessimages, pp. 12-13, 14-15, 18-19; Brocreative, p. 14 (students); Ground Picture, p. 16; skynesher, pp. 16-17; Ermolaeva Olga 84, pp. 20-21; M. Unal Ozmen, p. 22 (board); Nattstudio, p. 22 (lesson plan); ifong, p. 22 (computer); Dragon Images, p. 22 (plan lessons); AVAVA, p. 22 (grade work); martinedoucet, p. 23 (lessons).